HANDBOOK

Space

HANDBOOK

Space

Author: Sue Becklake
Consultant: Jerry Stone

Miles
KeLLY

First published in 2009 by
Miles Kelly Publishing Ltd,
Hardings Barn, Bardfield End Green,
Thaxted, Essex, CM6 3PX, UK

Copyright © Miles Kelly Publishing Ltd 2009

This edition printed in 2013

2 4 6 8 10 9 7 5 3 1

Publishing Director Belinda Gallagher
Creative Director Jo Cowan
Assistant Editor Sarah Parkin
Cover Designer Jo Cowan
Designer Michelle Foster
Image Manager Lorraine King
Production Manager Elizabeth Collins
Reprographics Stephan Davis,
Thom Allaway
Archive Manager Jennifer Hunt

ISBN 978-1-78209-166-0

Printed in China

British Library Cataloguing-in-Publication Data
A catalogue record for this book is available
from the British Library

Made with paper from a sustainable forest

www.mileskelly.net
info@mileskelly.net

www.factsforprojects.com

CONTENTS

WATCHING THE NIGHT SKY

It is easy to be a space detective from your own back garden. You will soon learn to pick out star patterns and how to spot planets, galaxies and satellites.

Where to watch

Find somewhere dark so you can see the stars clearly. If you live in the countryside away from city lights, your garden should be dark enough. Turn off the house lights and pick a spot with a clear view of the sky. If you live in the city, the lights swamp out the fainter stars, but you will be able to see the Moon and the brighter stars. You could ask an adult to take you to the countryside where the sky is darker, but do not go alone. Local astronomical societies often organize visits to good observing sites.

▶ *In a dark place, with a clear view of the sky, use a star map to spot the stars and constellations.*

When to watch

Choose a dark, clear night when there are no clouds and the Moon is not shining. You can spot stars at any time of year, but on winter nights the skies are darker earlier. Also, throughout the year there are different things to spot.

▲ Your eyes will stay adapted to the dark if you use a red torch.

Seeing in the dark

When you start watching, it takes about 20 minutes for your eyes to adapt to the dark. Gradually you will be able to see more and more stars. When your eyes are used to the dark, do not look at bright lights. Use a torch with a red light to look at a star chart.

What you need

The most important equipment to take with you is plenty of clothes to keep you warm outside at night. Sitting in a deck chair, wrapped in a blanket or a sleeping bag, is a comfortable way to star watch. A star chart or planisphere will show you which stars are in the sky.

Other useful items:

• A watch for making a note of the time

• A compass to find North, South, East and West, so you know in which direction you are looking

• A hot drink in a flask to help you keep warm

▶ Here are some things you may need when you are star-watching.

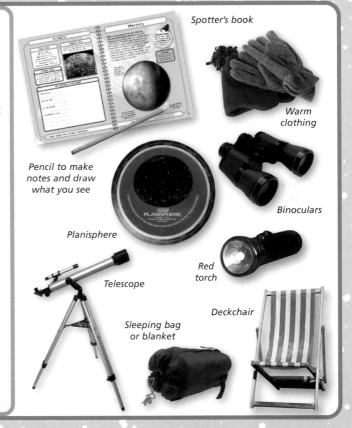

Spotter's book

Warm clothing

Pencil to make notes and draw what you see

Binoculars

Planisphere

Red torch

Telescope

Deckchair

Sleeping bag or blanket

SEEING FURTHER

You do not need special equipment to be a space detective. However, with binoculars or a telescope you will be able to see many more stars. They also make objects look nearer and larger, so you will see more details of the Moon and planets.

BINOCULARS

Using binoculars

A pair of telescopes mounted side by side, binoculars have lenses that capture more light, making things look brighter. Binoculars must be held very still to get a clear view. It is a good idea to rest them on something, such as the back of a chair, and use ones that are not

▲ With binoculars you will be able to see craters on the Moon and moons orbiting the planet Jupiter. It is easier to hold lightweight binoculars still and steady than big, heavy ones.

too heavy to hold steady. Binoculars are easier to use than a telescope when you start to become a space detective.

TELESCOPES

Using a telescope

One of the advantages of telescopes is that they are usually fixed to a tripod to keep them steady while viewing. You will generally see a smaller patch of sky through a telescope – you will have to move it around to follow the stars as they move across the sky.

Refracting telescope

There are two kinds of telescope – refracting and reflecting. Refracting telescopes use lenses to refract (bend) the light rays, just like binoculars.

▶ *Most early discoveries in astronomy were made with refracting telescopes.*

Reflecting telescope

The second kind of telescope is a reflecting telescope. This focuses light rays by reflecting them off curved mirrors. Reflecting telescopes bend the light rays back on themselves, so they are shorter than refracting rays and the telescopes are usually shorter and wider than refracting ones.

◀ *You often view through the side of a reflecting telescope tube.*

STARS ON THE MOVE

If you watch the night sky for an hour or two, you will notice that the stars have moved across the sky. The Sun also moves across the sky during the day. This happens because the Earth is constantly spinning.

Day and night

The Earth spins from West to East. During the day, the Sun travels across the sky from East to West. After it sets in the West, the sky is dark and we can see the stars. They are always there, but in the daytime the sunlight swamps out the faint starlight. At night, the star patterns also move across the sky from East to West, until they are hidden again by sunlight at dawn.

▲ A camera records trails showing the stars moving across the sky.

Celestial Sphere

Astronomers think of the stars as though they are fixed to a giant, imaginary ball surrounding the Earth.

They call this ball the Celestial Sphere and imagine that it rotates around the Earth, taking the stars with it.

▼ *The band around the Celestial Sphere, called the zodiac, shows the path of the Sun, Moon and planets across the sky.*

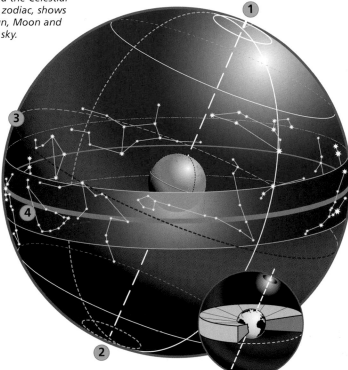

1 *Northern tip to North Celestial Pole*

2 *Southern tip to South Celestial Pole*

3 *Equator to Celestial Equator*

4 *Zodiac*

Plotting the stars

The stars each have their own place on the celestial sphere. Astronomers plot the positions of the stars on the sphere so they can find them easily.

Poles and equator

The points on the sphere above the Earth's North and South poles are called the Celestial North and South poles. A line around the middle of the sphere, above the Earth's equator, is called the Celestial Equator. The stars near the poles seem to move less than the stars near the Celestial Equator.

Astronomers use maps called star charts to find their way around the night sky. Each star is shown as a dot. The brighter stars have large dots and the fainter ones have small dots. Lines join up the dots to show the constellations.

Planisphere

A planisphere shows what stars are visible in the sky at different times throughout the year. It is a circular star chart with the months marked around the edge. Over this is a second rotating circle with an oval cut out and the hours of the day marked around the edge. Line up the date and time on the two circles and the oval hole reveals what is visible in the sky at that time.

▲ A planisphere shows the stars above your head when you face in the direction marked on it.

Measuring angles

It can be difficult to know how big the star patterns look in the sky compared with the star charts. Distances are measured in angles and your hand provides an easy way to measure angles in the sky. Holding your hand at arm's length, your closed fist is 10 degrees wide and your index finger is one degree. Compare this to the Moon, which is half a degree wide.

Light years

Kilometres are too small for measuring the vast distances to the stars, so astronomers use light years. One light year is the distance light travels in one year. This is 9.5 million million kilometres. The nearest star is 4.2 light years away.

Belt stars

Orion Nebula

Betelgeuse

Rigel

Orion Constellation

Distances to the stars

Each star is a different distance from the Earth. All stars are very far away but some are much further than others. Stars that look close together are often spread far apart.

▲ *This diagram shows the different distances to the stars in the constellation Orion.*

CONSTELLATIONS

Patterns made by the stars in the sky are called constellations. These patterns always stay the same. They have changed very little since ancient Greek and Roman astronomers mapped the stars thousands of years ago. Modern astronomers now divide the sky into 88 separate constellations.

Constellations of stars

The stars in each constellation are not linked or close together. Some are much further away than others, but we see them as a pattern in the sky because they all lie in the same direction. In each constellation, the stars are graded by their brightness using Greek letters. The brightest star is called Alpha, the first letter of the Greek alphabet, the second Beta and so on. Many bright stars also have their own names.

Naming constellations

Most of the constellations were named thousands of years ago by ancient astronomers. They called them after animals, such as a bear or a lion, or after heroes from their stories and legends. Most of the constellations look nothing like their names, so you have to use your imagination. They all have Latin names that have been translated into English. Some have nicknames that describe what they look like.

NORTHERN HEMISPHERE

The Northern Hemisphere is the half of the Earth that is North of the Equator.

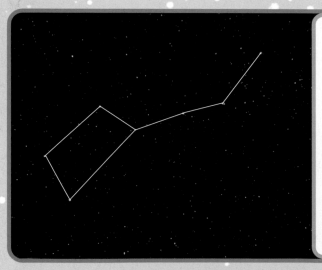

Star hopping

Constellations help you find your way around the night sky. When you have found one pattern of bright stars, you can use these as pointers to find a constellation nearby. In the Northern Hemisphere sky, a good starting point is the seven bright stars of the Plough, or Big Dipper.

◄ *Two bright stars in the Plough point to the Pole Star, which marks the North Celestial Pole.*

Ophiuchus
(Serpent Bearer)

Aquila
(Eagle)

Serpens
(Serpent)

Hercules
(Strongman)

Sagitta
(Arrow)

Equuleus
(Foal)

Corona Borealis
(Northern Crown)

Lyra
(Lyre)

Boótes
(Herdsman)

Delphinus
(Dolphin)

Draco
(Dragon)

Cygnus
(Swan)

Pegasus
(Winged Horse)

Coma Berenices
(Berenice's Hair)

Lacerta
(Lizard)

Virgo
(Virgin)

Canes Venatici
(Hunting Dogs)

Cepheus
(King)

Andromeda
(Chained
Princess)

Pisces
(Fishes)

Ursa Minor
(Little Bear)

Leo
(Lion)

Ursa Major
(Great Bear)

Cassiopeia
(Queen)

Triangulum
(Triangle)

Leo Minor
(Little Lion)

Camelopardalis
(Giraffe)

Cancer
(Crab)

Lynx (Lynx)

Perseus
(Hero)

Aries
(Ram)

Hydra
(Sea Serpent)

Auriga
(Charioteer)

Cetus
(Whale)

Gemini
(Twins)

Taurus (Bull)

Canis Minor
(Little Dog)

Orion
(Hunter)

▲ The constellations around the
edge of the chart can be seen
from both the Northern and the
Southern hemispheres.

SOUTHERN HEMISPHERE

The Southern Hemisphere is the half of the Earth that is South of the Equator. If you live in the Southern Hemisphere, you will never be able to see the constellations near the North Celestial Pole. Similarly, if you live in the Northern Hemisphere, the constellations near the South Celestial Pole are always hidden from view.

Round the Equator

If you live near the Equator you will be able to see all of the constellations, but not at the same time. The earth beneath your feet blocks the view of half the sky. During a whole year, as the Earth moves around the Sun, you will get the chance to see every constellation in the sky.

Exploring the southern skies

Astronomers in Europe and Asia (North of the Equator) did not have any maps of the stars near the South Celestial Pole until explorers first sailed south of the Equator nearly 500 years ago. They then added new constellations to the original list of 48 that had been named by the ancient Greeks. The constellations are not all the same size – some are much bigger than others. The largest constellation is Hydra and the smallest is Crux. They also vary in brightness – Orion's bright stars make it easy to spot, but Cancer has mostly faint stars and is more difficult to find.

Southern star hopping

Star hopping in the South often starts with four stars in the shape of a cross, called Crux, which is easy to find. However, there is no bright star marking the South Pole. The southern skies seem to be crammed with bright stars compared with the northern skies.

▶ *Crux can always be seen in the southern skies. It points towards the South Pole and lies in the Milky Way galaxy.*

Lepus
(Hare)

Canis Major
(Great Dog)

Columba
(Dove)

Eridanus
(River Eridanus)

Puppis (Stern), Carina (Keel)
and Vela (Sail)

Caelum
(Chisel)

Fornax
(Furnace)

Pictor
(Painter's Easel)

Sextans
(Sextant)

Hydra
(Sea Serpent)

Recticulum
(Net)

Dorado
(Goldfish)

Phoenix
(Phoenix)

Cetus
(Whale)

Crater
(Cup)

Volans (Flying Fish)

Crux
(Southern
Cross)

Chamaeleon
(Chameleon)

Grus (Crane),
Tucana (Toucan),
and Pavo (Peacock)

Corvus
(Crow)

Centaurus
(Centaur)

Musca
(Fly)

Apus
(Bird of
Paradise)

Virgo
(Virgin)

Indus
(Indian)

Aquarius
(Water
Carrier)

Triangulum Australe
(Southern Triangle)

Piscis Austrinus
(Southern Fish)

Ara (Altar)

Corona Australis
(Southern Crown)

Scorpius
(Scorpion)

Capricornus
(Sea Goat)

Libra
(Scales)

Serpens (Serpent) and
Ophiuchus (Serpent Bearer)

Sagittarius
(Archer)

▲ From the Southern
Hemisphere, you can see the
stars near the middle of this
chart all the year round.

HOW TO FIND THE PLANETS

The planets sometimes shine brightly and are very obvious in the sky. At other times they can be difficult to find – They move across the patterns made by the stars, so you need to know where to look for them.

Orbiting planets

All the planets orbit (travel around) the Sun and each travels at a different speed. Mercury is nearest the Sun and completes one orbit in only 88 days. Saturn takes over 29 years to go around the Sun once. Because the Earth also moves around the Sun, it is not an easy task to work out where and when to look for each planet. Luckily, astronomers have done this for you and newspapers, astronomical magazines and websites will provide details of when each planet is visible (see page 94 to find out more).

▲ Planets shine by reflecting sunlight, so those nearest the Sun shine brightest. The planet closest to the Sun is Mercury, followed by Venus, Earth, Mars, Jupiter, Saturn, Uranus and Neptune.

Only five planets

Although there are eight main planets, including Earth, in the Solar System, only five can be spotted in the sky with the naked eye. The two planets furthest from the Sun, Uranus and Neptune, are too faint and far away to see.

◀ Venus can be brighter than any star or other planet.

▶ Jupiter is the largest planet, but not as bright as Venus.

Zodiac

The orbits of the planets all lie in a flat disc around the Sun. So when you see them, they are always in a narrow band around the sky. This band goes through 12 constellations, which together are called the zodiac. The constellations of the zodiac are Capricorn, Aquarius, Pisces, Aries, Taurus, Gemini, Cancer, Leo, Virgo, Libra, Scorpius and Sagittarius.

▼ *During one year the Sun goes though each of the constellations of the zodiac.*

Capricorn

Aquarius

Pisces

Aries

Taurus

Gemini

Cancer

Leo

Virgo

Libra

Scorpius

Sagittarius

HOW TO STUDY THE SUN SAFELY

You cannot study the Sun by looking at it directly. However, you can safely look at an image of the Sun made with binoculars or a telescope. You should always ask an adult to help you do this.

Making an image with a telescope

You need a telescope and two screens – white cardboard will do. Cut a hole in one sheet so it fits around the telescope eyepiece. Point the telescope towards the Sun without looking through it or the finder scope – keep a lens cap on the finder scope. Put the second piece of card in the shadow of the first. Tilt the telescope until you can see an image of the Sun on this screen.

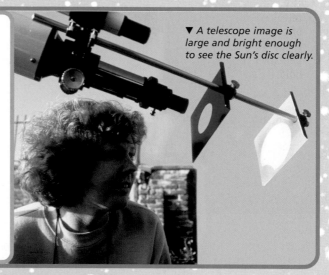

▼ *A telescope image is large and bright enough to see the Sun's disc clearly.*

Viewing an eclipse of the Sun

Projected images of the Sun safely show an eclipse (see pages 34–35) or even sunspots on the Sun (see pages 32–33). Focus the telescope to get a clear image and move the screen further away to make the image larger, but fainter.

◄ *Use a sheet of white card as a screen for watching an eclipse of the Sun.*

Making an image with binoculars

You can also use binoculars to look at the Sun. Use only one of the binocular lenses and keep the other covered with a lens cap. Fix one piece of card around the eyepiece to cast a shadow and look for an image on the other card.

Pinhole viewer

If you don't have binoculars or a telescope, you can make a small image of the Sun using two pieces of card. Make a small hole using the point of a pencil in the first piece of card. Then hold it facing the Sun, so that its shadow falls on the second card. Start with the cards close together and look for a small, bright spot of light on the second card. If you move the cards further apart, the image of the Sun will get bigger, but less bright.

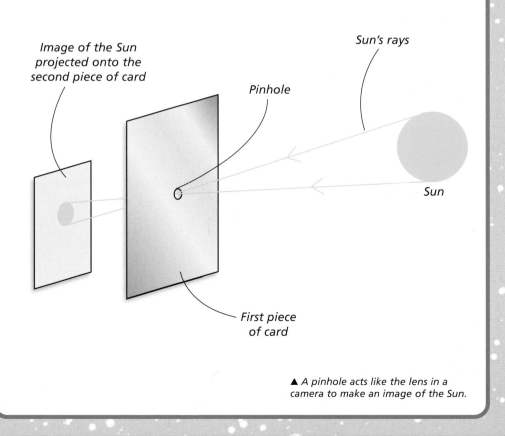

Image of the Sun projected onto the second piece of card

Pinhole

Sun's rays

Sun

First piece of card

▲ *A pinhole acts like the lens in a camera to make an image of the Sun.*

HOW TO USE THIS BOOK

Use this guide to help you find your way around this book. There's information about all kinds of space objects, plus amazing facts, key spotting times and photo files. You can add your own notes and pictures in the write-in areas and record your sightings on the bars.

Photo file
See a close-up of objects in space, such as planets and comets.

Fact file
Packed with essential dates, times and facts.

Super fact
Find out lots of amazing facts about space.

Write-in area
Draw pictures, take photos and add notes and thoughts about anything you see.

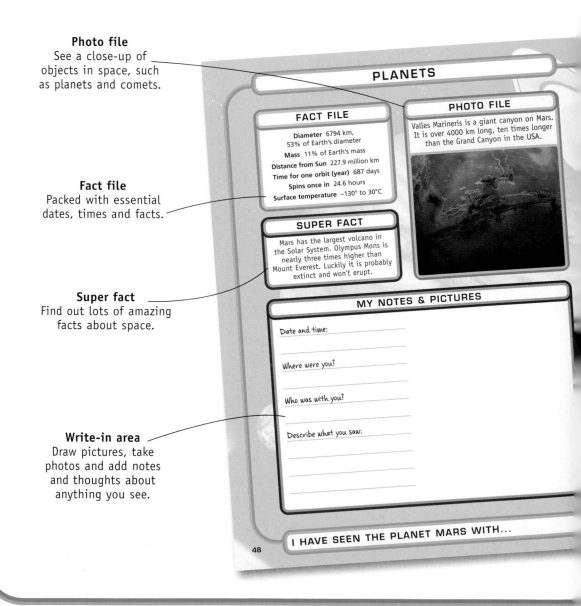

PLANETS

FACT FILE

Diameter 6794 km, 53% of Earth's diameter
Mass 11% of Earth's mass
Distance from Sun 227.9 million km
Time for one orbit (year) 687 days
Spins once in 24.6 hours
Surface temperature −130° to 30°C

PHOTO FILE

Valles Marineris is a giant canyon on Mars. It is over 4000 km long, ten times longer than the Grand Canyon in the USA.

SUPER FACT

Mars has the largest volcano in the Solar System. Olympus Mons is nearly three times higher than Mount Everest. Luckily it is probably extinct and won't erupt.

MY NOTES & PICTURES

Date and time:

Where were you?

Who was with you?

Describe what you saw:

I HAVE SEEN THE PLANET MARS WITH...

48

WEB LINK

Visit **www.factsforprojects.com** for links to websites where you can learn more about space and find images, facts, videos and activities.

Mars

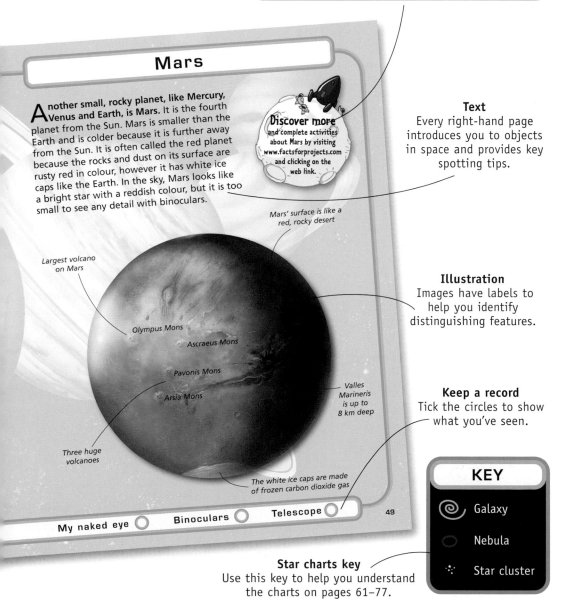

Another small, rocky planet, like Mercury, Venus and Earth, is Mars. It is the fourth planet from the Sun. Mars is smaller than the Earth and is colder because it is further away from the Sun. It is often called the red planet because the rocks and dust on its surface are rusty red in colour, however it has white ice caps like the Earth. In the sky, Mars looks like a bright star with a reddish colour, but it is too small to see any detail with binoculars.

Discover more and complete activities about Mars by visiting www.factsforprojects.com and clicking on the web link.

Mars' surface is like a red, rocky desert

Largest volcano on Mars

Olympus Mons

Ascraeus Mons

Pavonis Mons

Arsia Mons

Valles Marineris is up to 8 km deep

Three huge volcanoes

The white ice caps are made of frozen carbon dioxide gas

My naked eye ◯   Binoculars ◯   Telescope ◯   49

Text
Every right-hand page introduces you to objects in space and provides key spotting tips.

Illustration
Images have labels to help you identify distinguishing features.

Keep a record
Tick the circles to show what you've seen.

KEY

🌀 Galaxy

◯ Nebula

∴ Star cluster

Star charts key
Use this key to help you understand the charts on pages 61–77.

23

THE SUN'S FAMILY

The Earth we live on is a huge ball of rock whirling through space. It is one of a family of eight planets, all circling around the Sun. This family is called the Solar System and it also includes moons, comets and asteroids.

Planets

The four planets nearest to the Sun, Mercury, Venus, Earth and Mars, are all small and rocky. Those further away, Jupiter, Saturn, Uranus and Neptune, are much bigger and made mostly of gas and liquid. The biggest planet is Jupiter and the smallest is Mercury. Smaller planets, such as Pluto, are called dwarf planets.

1 Mercury   5 Jupiter

2 Venus   6 Saturn

3 Earth   7 Uranus

4 Mars   8 Neptune

▼ In this image, the sizes of the planets are shown to scale, but they are all much further apart than this.

Sun

Moons

Planets are circled by moons. All the planets, except Mercury and Venus, have their own moons. Jupiter and Saturn both have more than 60 moons, but most of these are very small and icy. The Earth's moon is one of the biggest.

▶ *The Moon is smaller than Earth, with no air or water.*

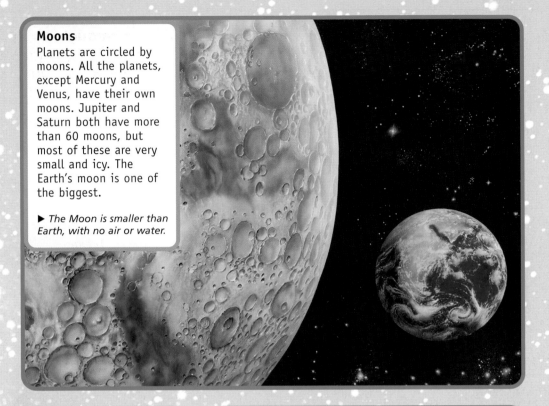

Never still

Everything in the Solar System is moving. Planets, asteroids and comets hurtle around the Sun and moons whiz around the planets. Their paths through space are called orbits. All these objects are also spinning around. Even the Sun spins and moves through space, taking the Solar System with it.

▶ *The asteroids in the asteroid belt all orbit the Sun like tiny planets.*

Asteroids and comets

There are millions of asteroids in a band called the asteroid belt between Mars and Jupiter. Asteroids are rocky chunks of all shapes and sizes. Comets are a mixture of dust and ice. Most of them are far away from the Sun. When a comet does come close to the Sun, it can develop a huge tail.

Jupiter

Mars

Asteroid belt

STARS

Stars are enormous balls of hot, glowing gas. The Sun is a star, but it looks much larger than all of the other stars because it is much closer to Earth.

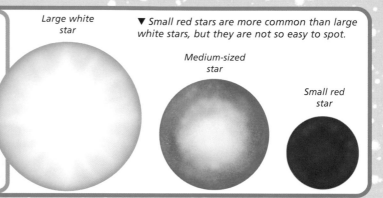

Colours and sizes

Stars vary enormously in size and temperature. They can also display a wide range of colours. The Sun is a medium-sized star and looks yellow in colour.

Large white star

▼ Small red stars are more common than large white stars, but they are not so easy to spot.

Medium-sized star

Small red star

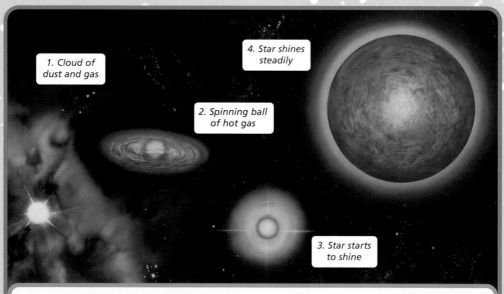

1. Cloud of dust and gas

4. Star shines steadily

2. Spinning ball of hot gas

3. Star starts to shine

Life of a star

Stars do not last forever. They start life in a cloud of dust and gas, where thicker clumps squash into balls, getting smaller and hotter until they shine as stars.

▲ Stars form together in dusty clouds and most spend their lives in pairs or groups.

A medium-sized star, such as the Sun, will shine for billions of years. Giant stars shine very brightly, but have much shorter lives.

Death of a star

When stars can no longer make energy they swell up into cooler, red giant stars. They then lose their outer layers, leaving a small, hot, white dwarf star, that gradually cools and dies. Giant stars may end in a huge explosion called a supernova. This leaves a very small neutron star or a black hole.

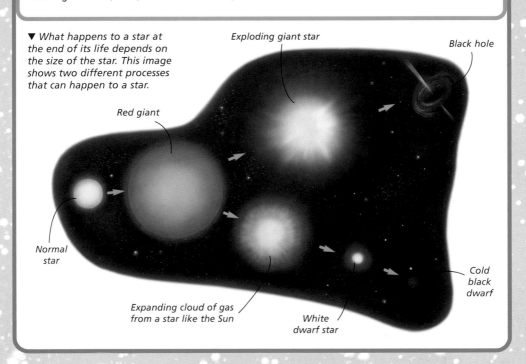

▼ What happens to a star at the end of its life depends on the size of the star. This image shows two different processes that can happen to a star.

Exploding giant star

Black hole

Red giant

Normal star

Expanding cloud of gas from a star like the Sun

White dwarf star

Cold black dwarf

Energy from stars

Stars shine because they make energy. In the centre of the star, gas presses down so hard that nuclear reactions change some of the gas into energy. This energy moves slowly out to the surface, where it escapes as heat and light.

Changing stars

Not all stars shine steadily. Some look brighter, then dimmer as they swell up then contract. Others look dimmer when their light is blocked by a companion star.

◄ Stars that do not shine steadily are called variable stars.

NEBULAE

A nebula (plural nebulae) is a cloud of dust and gas in space in between stars. Some of these clouds are where new stars are born and others are created when stars die. At the end of their lives, dying stars throw out a cloud of dust and gas around them.

Bright nebulae

Most of the gas and dust in space is invisible because it does not give out any light. We can only see it when light from a nearby star makes the gas glow in bright colours. Both newborn and dying stars make the gas around them glow.

▼ *Bright stars make the gas in the Trifid Nebula glow red.*

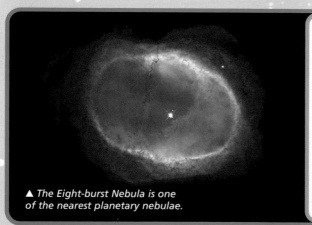

▲ *The Eight-burst Nebula is one of the nearest planetary nebulae.*

Planetary nebulae

When stars die their outer layers expand out into space, making a cloud of gas and dust around the star. Light from the star makes this glow as a planetary nebula (this has nothing to do with planets – early astronomers just thought they looked like planets). Exploding stars throw out a cloud of gas and dust called a supernova remnant.

Dark nebulae

Some nebulae show up as dark shadows. This happens when thick clouds of dust and gas block out light from a bright nebula behind it.

▶ *The Horsehead Nebula gets its name from its shape. It is a dark dust cloud silhouetted against a glowing, pink gas cloud.*

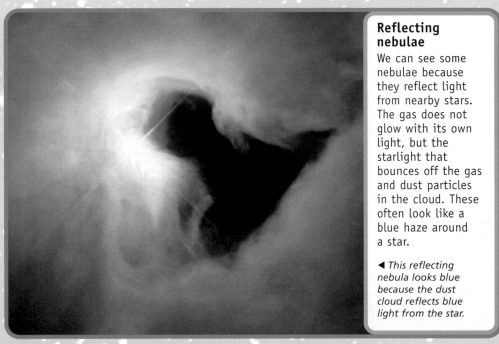

Reflecting nebulae

We can see some nebulae because they reflect light from nearby stars. The gas does not glow with its own light, but the starlight that bounces off the gas and dust particles in the cloud. These often look like a blue haze around a star.

◀ *This reflecting nebula looks blue because the dust cloud reflects blue light from the star.*

GALAXIES

Stars are not spread evenly through space – they group together **in huge families called galaxies.** The Sun belongs to an enormous galaxy of between 200 and 400 billion stars called the Milky Way.

Spiral galaxies

Many galaxies have a spiral shape with a tight bulge of stars in the middle. Spiral arms curl outwards from the bulge in a flat disc shape. The Milky Way is a spiral galaxy with the Sun in one of the spiral arms, about two-thirds of the way out from the centre. From Earth we cannot see its spiral shape, just a band of light from billions of other stars in our galaxy.

▲ *This is what the Milky Way would look like from outside.*

Irregular and elliptical galaxies

Some galaxies do not have any definite shape at all – these are called irregular galaxies. Elliptical galaxies are in the shape of a squashed ball. They can be quite small, with only about ten million stars, or giants much larger than our galaxy, with thousands of billions of stars.

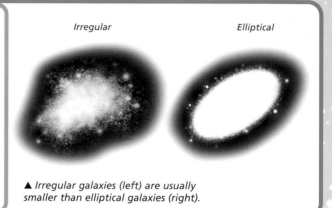

Irregular   *Elliptical*

▲ *Irregular galaxies (left) are usually smaller than elliptical galaxies (right).*

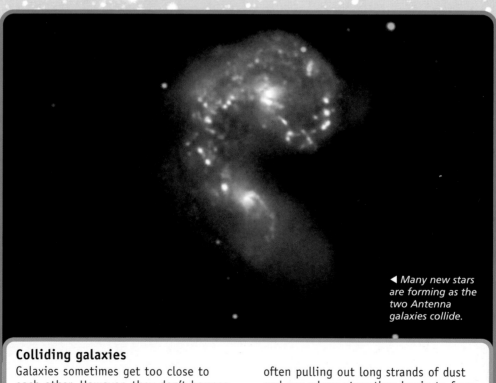

◄ *Many new stars are forming as the two Antenna galaxies collide.*

Colliding galaxies

Galaxies sometimes get too close to each other. However, they don't bounce off each other when they collide because they are mostly empty space. Instead they may pull each other out of shape, often pulling out long strands of dust and gas where stars then begin to form. In some cases, a large galaxy will become a cannibal and completely swallow up a smaller one.

THE SUN

FACT FILE

Average temperature of sunspot
4000°C

Temperature of Sun's surface 5500°C

Size of smallest sunspots
About 300 km across

Size of largest sunspots
About ten times Earth's diameter

PHOTO FILE

This shows a group of sunspots close-up. The dark, central parts are 1500°C cooler than the rest of the Sun's surface.

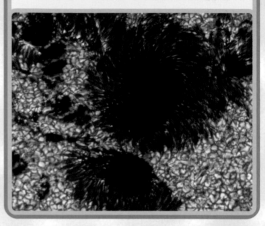

SUPER FACT

No sunspots were seen for 70 years between 1645–1715. This time was called the Little Ice Age – the winters on Earth were very cold and the river Thames in London froze.

MY NOTES & PICTURES

Date and time:

Where were you?

Who was with you?

Describe what you saw:

I HAVE SEEN... **A projected image of the Sun**

Sunspots

If you project an image of the Sun using binoculars or a telescope (see pages 20–21), you may be able to see some dark spots on the Sun. These are called sunspots. They are slightly cooler than the rest of the Sun, although they are still extremely hot. Look again on the next sunny day and you will see that the sunspots have moved across the Sun. This is because the Sun rotates over a period of 28 days. The number of spots on the Sun varies with a peak every 11 years.

Learn how to project an image of the Sun by visiting www.factsforprojects.com and clicking on the web link.

Warning: Never look at the Sun without equipment specifically designed for that purpose. Sunlight can damage your eyes or even make you blind.

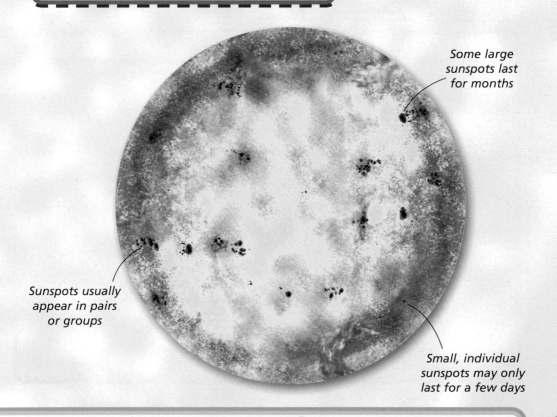

Some large sunspots last for months

Sunspots usually appear in pairs or groups

Small, individual sunspots may only last for a few days

THE SUN

FACT FILE

FUTURE TOTAL SOLAR ECLIPSES

When	Where
03.11.2013	Eastern Americas, S. Europe, Africa
20.03.2015	North Atlantic Ocean, Norwegian Sea, Svalbard
09.03.2016	Indonesia, North Pacific Ocean

PHOTO FILE

This image shows the Moon's shadow on Earth from space. People in the shadow see a total eclipse of the Sun.

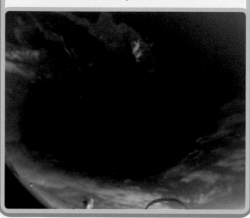

SUPER FACT

The Sun and Moon appear to be exactly the same size in the sky. The Sun is really 400 times larger than the Moon, but it is also 400 times further away.

MY NOTES & PICTURES

Date and time:

Where were you?

Who was with you?

Describe what you saw:

I HAVE SEEN A... Total eclipse of the Sun ◯

Solar Eclipse

Sometimes the Sun, Moon and Earth all line up so that the Moon is directly in front of the Sun. The Moon blocks out the sunlight and its shadow, only a few kilometres wide, falls on the Earth. This is called an eclipse of the Sun. If you are in the shadow you will see a total eclipse – the Sun completely disappears for a few minutes. Just outside the shadow you will see the Moon covering part of the Sun – this is a partial eclipse.

Discover how to make a pinhole viewer by visiting www.factsforprojects.com and clicking on the web link.

Warning: Only watch an eclipse of the Sun by projecting an image (onto paper or card), or by using special filters that allow you to watch an eclipse safely.

The Sun's corona, a ring of white glowing gas, is only seen during an eclipse

The Moon completely covers the Sun in a total eclipse

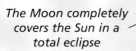

Partial eclipse of the Sun

THE EARTH'S MOON

FACT FILE

Diameter 3476 km,
27% of Earth's diameter

Mass 1.2% of Earth's mass

Distance from Earth 384,400 km

Time for one orbit of Earth
27.3 days

Spins once in 27.3 days

SUPER FACT

People used to believe that a Full Moon could send some people mad. The word 'lunatic' comes from the Latin word 'luna', meaning Moon.

PHOTO FILE

You will see the Crescent Moon in the West just after the Sun has set, or in the East just before the Sun rises.

MY NOTES & PICTURES

Date and time:

Where were you?

Who was with you?

Describe what you saw:

I HAVE SEEN A...   New Moon    Crescent Moon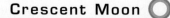

Phases of the Moon

Watch the Moon for a month and you will see it change shape from a Full Moon to a thin, crescent shape. These are the phases of the Moon. It does not change shape – as it circles the Earth we can only see the part of Moon that is lit by the Sun. When the whole of the sunlit side faces the Earth there is a Full Moon. When the sunlit side is facing away from Earth, we cannot see it at all and there is a New Moon.

Complete a quiz about the phases of the Moon by visiting www.factsforprojects.com and clicking on the web link.

During the first half of each monthly cycle, the Moon waxes (grows) from a crescent-shaped New Moon (2) to a Full Moon (5)

3 *Half Moon*

4 *Gibbous Moon*

2 *Crescent Moon*

5 *Full Moon*
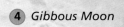

1 *New Moon*

6 *Gibbous Moon*

8 *Crescent Moon*

7 *Half Moon*

During the second half, the Moon wanes (dwindles) back to a crescent-shaped Old Moon (8)

Half Moon ◯   Gibbous Moon ◯   Full Moon ◯

THE EARTH'S MOON

FACT FILE

FUTURE TOTAL LUNAR ECLIPSES

- 15.04.2014
- 08.10.2014
- 04.04.2015
- 28.09.2015
- 31.01.2018
- 27.07.2018
- 21.01.2019
- 26.05.2021

PHOTO FILE

During a lunar eclipse the Moon turns reddish in colour, because sunlight is bent by the Earth's atmosphere onto the Moon.

SUPER FACT

There is not an eclipse every time there is a Full Moon because the Moon's orbit is tilted. Mostly, the Moon goes above or below the Earth's shadow, not through it.

MY NOTES & PICTURES

Date and time:

_____

Where were you?

_____

Who was with you?

_____

Describe what you saw:

_____

_____

_____

I HAVE SEEN A... Total eclipse of the Moon

Lunar Eclipse

An eclipse of the Moon happens when the Sun, Earth and Moon are lined up. The Moon passes through the Earth's shadow as it orbits the Earth. If the whole Moon goes into the shadow there is a total eclipse. If only part of the Moon goes into the shadow there is a partial eclipse. An eclipse of the Moon can only happen when there is a Full Moon and can last for over an hour. It can be seen from anywhere on Earth where it is night time.

Watch a video of a lunar eclipse by visiting www.factsforprojects.com and clicking on the web link.

1   **2**   **3**   **4**   **5**

The changing appearance of the Moon at different stages during an eclipse.

1 The Moon moves into the Earth's shadow at the start of an eclipse

2 Partial eclipse with most of the Moon in shadow

3 Total eclipse

4 Moving out of the shadow

5 Eclipse almost ended

Partial eclipse of the Moon

THE EARTH'S MOON

FACT FILE

DIAMETERS OF SEAS

Sea of Crises	418 km
Sea of Serenity	707 km
Sea of Clouds	715 km
Sea of Tranquility	873 km
Sea of Showers	1123 km

PHOTO FILE

The Full Moon always looks the same because the same side of the Moon always faces the Earth.

SUPER FACT

The Moon spins around in exactly the same time as it takes to orbit the Earth, so we can never see the farside of the Moon from Earth.

MY NOTES & PICTURES

Date and time:

Where were you?

Who was with you?

Describe what you saw:

I HAVE SEEN THE SEAS OF... Tranquility Serenity

Seas on the Moon

When you look at the Moon you can see **dark and light patches.** The darker parts are low, flat plains. People used to think that these were oceans and they called them 'seas'. We now know that the seas are actually completely dry. They are the remains of huge craters made when giant space rocks crashed into the Moon. Melted rock leaked out from inside the Moon and covered the floors of the craters with darker rock. You will be able to pick out individual seas using binoculars.

Learn more and complete activities about the Moon by visiting www.factsforprojects.com and clicking on the web link.

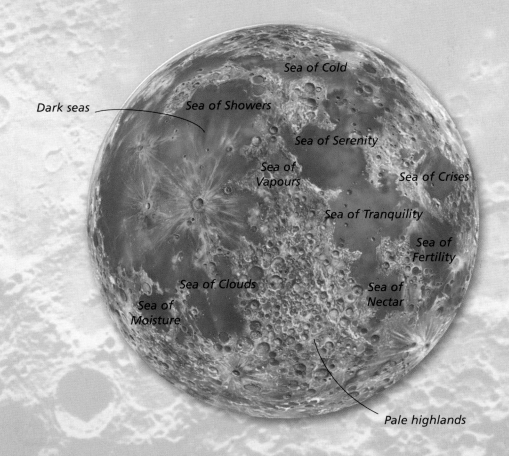

Sea of Cold

Dark seas

Sea of Showers

Sea of Serenity

Sea of Vapours

Sea of Crises

Sea of Tranquility

Sea of Fertility

Sea of Clouds

Sea of Nectar

Sea of Moisture

Pale highlands

THE EARTH'S MOON

FACT FILE

DIAMETERS OF CRATERS

Archimedes	82 km
Tycho	102 km
Copernicus	107 km
Plato	109 km
Ptolemy	164 km

PHOTO FILE

Near the line between the dark and light parts of the Moon, the shadows are long and craters show up more clearly.

SUPER FACT

The largest crater on the Moon is called the South Pole-Aitken Basin, discovered in 1962. It is on the farside of the Moon and is 2500 km wide and over 12 km deep.

MY NOTES & PICTURES

Date and time:

_____

Where were you?

_____

Who was with you?

_____

Describe what you saw:

_____

_____

_____

I HAVE SEEN THE CRATERS... Tycho Copernicus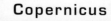

Craters on the Moon

The Moon is covered in round scars called craters. They were made billions of years ago by space rocks crashing onto the Moon's surface. The biggest craters are hundreds of kilometres wide. With binoculars you will be able to see some of these. The best time to look for craters is when there is a Half Moon. Some craters are surrounded by streaks called rays – you will see these best when there is a Full Moon. Most craters are circular, with a dip in the middle, and are surrounded by a ring of mountains.

Discover how to make your own crater by visiting www.factsforprojects.com and clicking on the web link.

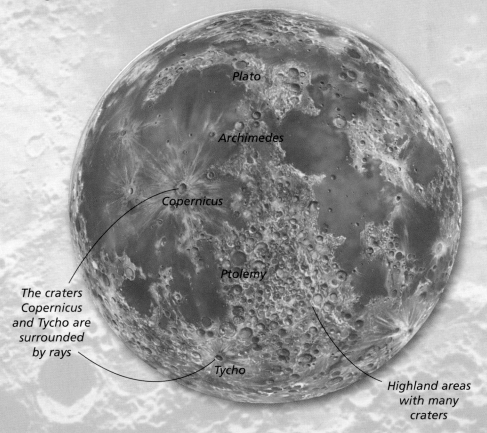

Plato

Archimedes

Copernicus

Ptolemy

The craters Copernicus and Tycho are surrounded by rays

Tycho

Highland areas with many craters

PLANETS

FACT FILE

Diameter 4879 km,
38% of Earth's diameter
Mass 5.5% of Earth's mass
Distance from Sun 57.9 million km
Time for one orbit (year) 88 days
Spins once in 58.6 days
Surface temperature −180° to 430°C

SUPER FACT

Mercury's day is twice as long as its year. It spins once in nearly 59 days, but the time from one sunrise to the next is 176 days because it orbits the Sun in only 88 days.

PHOTO FILE

Close-up pictures taken by the Mariner 10 space probe show Mercury's rocky surface with hundreds of craters.

MY NOTES & PICTURES

Date and time:

Where were you?

Who was with you?

Describe what you saw:

I HAVE SEEN THE PLANET MERCURY...

Mercury

The closest planet to the Sun, Mercury is also the smallest planet. It is very hot because it is so close to the Sun – temperatures reach 430°C during the day. However, at night, the side that faces away from the Sun gets colder than the lowest temperatures on Earth – it can reach as low as –180°C. Mercury is difficult to spot in the sky because it is so close to the Sun. Look for it just after sunset, near the horizon where the Sun has set, or in the morning just before sunrise.

Discover more and complete activities about Mercury by visiting www.factsforprojects.com and clicking on the web link.

Warning:
Never look at Mercury with binoculars or a telescope – it is too close to the Sun.

The largest crater, called the Caloris Basin, is 1550 km wide and 2 km deep

Mercury is deeply dented with craters made by space debris crashing into it

Mercury's surface is wrinkled by long, high ridges

After sunset ○   Before sunrise ○

FACT FILE

Diameter 12,104 km,
95% of Earth's diameter

Mass 82% of Earth's mass

Distance from Sun 108.2 million km

Time for one orbit (year) 225 days

Spins once in 243 days

Surface temperature 465°C

PHOTO FILE

This picture of the volcano Maat Mons was made by the Magellan space probe, using radar to see through Venus' thick clouds.

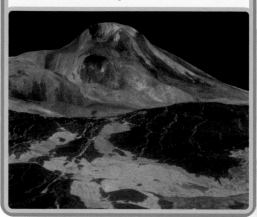

SUPER FACT

It is very difficult to land on Venus. Surface clouds trap heat making the planet hotter than an oven. Venus' atmosphere presses down 90 times harder than the air on Earth.

MY NOTES & PICTURES

Date and time:

Where were you?

Who was with you?

Describe what you saw:

I HAVE SEEN THE PLANET VENUS WITH...

Venus

The second planet from the Sun is Venus. It is about the same size as the Earth and is covered with thick clouds. Venus is the brightest object in the night sky apart from the Moon. It is often called the Evening or Morning Star because it shines brightly in the western sky soon after sunset, or in the eastern sky just before dawn. Venus has phases like the Moon – if you look at it with binoculars you may see a crescent shape.

Learn more and complete activities about Venus by visiting www.factsforprojects.com and clicking on the web link.

Space probes that landed on Venus found a dry, rocky surface

Venus' surface is completely hidden by thick clouds

Venus is the hottest planet because its clouds trap the heat

The clouds contain acid that could burn your skin

My naked eye ◯   Binoculars ◯   Telescope ◯

PLANETS

FACT FILE

Diameter 6794 km,
53% of Earth's diameter
Mass 11% of Earth's mass
Distance from Sun 227.9 million km
Time for one orbit (year) 687 days
Spins once in 24.6 hours
Surface temperature −130° to 30°C

SUPER FACT

Mars has the largest volcano in the Solar System. Olympus Mons is nearly three times higher than Mount Everest. Luckily it is probably extinct and won't erupt.

PHOTO FILE

Valles Marineris is a giant canyon on Mars. It is over 4000 km long, ten times longer than the Grand Canyon in the USA.

MY NOTES & PICTURES

Date and time:

Where were you?

Who was with you?

Describe what you saw:

I HAVE SEEN THE PLANET MARS WITH...

Mars

Another small, rocky planet, like Mercury, Venus and Earth, is Mars. It is the fourth planet from the Sun. Mars is smaller than the Earth and is colder because it is further away from the Sun. It is often called the red planet because the rocks and dust on its surface are rusty red in colour, however it has white ice caps like the Earth. In the sky, Mars looks like a bright star with a reddish colour, but it is too small to see any detail with binoculars.

Discover more and complete activities about Mars by visiting www.factsforprojects.com and clicking on the web link.

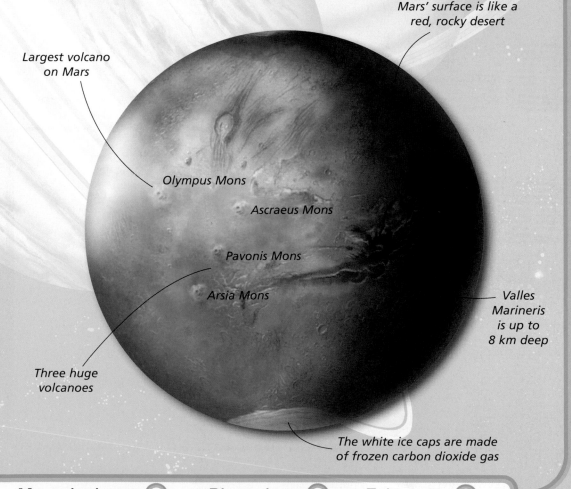

Largest volcano on Mars

Mars' surface is like a red, rocky desert

Olympus Mons

Ascraeus Mons

Pavonis Mons

Arsia Mons

Valles Marineris is up to 8 km deep

Three huge volcanoes

The white ice caps are made of frozen carbon dioxide gas

My naked eye ⃝　　Binoculars ⃝　　Telescope ⃝

FACT FILE

Diameter 142,984 km,
11.2 times Earth's diameter

Mass 318 times Earth's mass

Distance from Sun 778.3 million km

Time for one orbit (year) 11.86 years

Spins once in 9.9 hours

Surface temperature −140°C

SUPER FACT

Jupiter spins so fast that it bulges out around the middle. Its speedy spin makes the colourful clouds stretch out into orange and yellow bands around the planet.

PHOTO FILE

Io, one of Jupiter's four large moons, has volcanoes that throw plumes of melted rock high above the yellowish surface.

MY NOTES & PICTURES

Date and time:

Where were you?

Who was with you?

Describe what you saw:

I HAVE SEEN THE PLANET JUPITER WITH...

Jupiter

The biggest planet in the Solar System, Jupiter's mass is larger than all the other planets put together. It is the fifth planet from the Sun. Jupiter is called a gas giant because it is made of gas and liquid, with a small rocky core hidden deep in the middle. It looks like a bright white star in the sky. With binoculars you may be able to spot its four largest moons as tiny dots on either side of the planet. They change places on different nights as they move around Jupiter.

Find out more and complete activities about Jupiter by visiting www.factsforprojects.com and clicking on the web link.

Fierce winds swirl Jupiter's clouds into oval storms

Light stripes are called zones

Bands of different-coloured clouds stretch around Jupiter

Dark stripes are called belts

The Great Red Spot is a huge whirling storm larger than the Earth

My naked eye ○   Binoculars ○   Telescope ○

PLANETS

FACT FILE

Diameter 120,536 km,
9.45 times Earth's diameter

Mass 95 times Earth's mass

Distance from Sun 1433 million km

Time for one orbit (year) 29.66 years

Spins once in 10.65 hours

Surface temperature −180°C

SUPER FACT

Saturn's rings shine brilliantly because they are made of billions of small, icy chunks all orbiting the planet. Some are as small as an ice cube and others the size of a car.

PHOTO FILE

A close-up view of Saturn's rings from the Voyager space probe show thousands of separate rings around the planet.

MY NOTES & PICTURES

Date and time:

Where were you?

Who was with you?

Describe what you saw:

I HAVE SEEN THE PLANET SATURN WITH...

Saturn

Another gas giant planet, Saturn is almost as large as Jupiter but nearly twice as far from the Sun. It is the sixth planet from the Sun. Saturn's clouds are not as bright as Jupiter's, but it makes up for this with its spectacular rings, which stretch out in a disc around its equator (an imaginary line around the centre of the planet). The rings are too far away to see clearly with binoculars – you need a telescope. Saturn looks like a bright-yellow star in the sky. It is the faintest of the planets you can see with the naked eye.

Learn more and complete activities about Saturn by visiting www.factsforprojects.com and clicking on the web link.

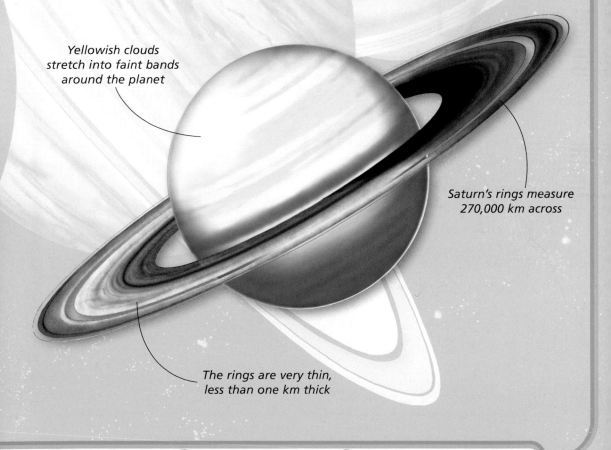

Yellowish clouds stretch into faint bands around the planet

Saturn's rings measure 270,000 km across

The rings are very thin, less than one km thick

My naked eye ◯   Binoculars ◯   Telescope ◯

SPACE ROCKS

FACT FILE

Typical size of nucleus 1–10 km

Typical length of tail Up to 150 million km

TYPES OF COMET

Periodic Take less than 200 years to orbit the Sun

Long period Take longer than 200 years for one orbit

SUPER FACT

Halley's comet is named after Edmund Halley (1656–1742). He predicted that it would return in 1758. It was the first time a comet's arrival had been predicted.

PHOTO FILE

Comet Hale-Bopp was seen shining brightly for several months in 1997. It will return to the Sun in 2400 years time.

MY NOTES & PICTURES

Date and time:

Where were you?

Who was with you?

Describe what you saw:

I HAVE SEEN A COMET WITH...

Comets

Often described as dirty snowballs, comets are small chunks made of ice and dust. They are usually too small and far away to be seen, even by powerful telescopes. When a comet comes close to the Sun, the ice melts, forming a giant, glowing tail of gas and dust. This is what we see in the sky. Some comets reappear regularly, such as the famous Halley's Comet, which orbits the Sun every 76 years. Others turn up unexpectedly. Bright comets that can be seen with the naked eye are rare.

Discover more about comets by visiting www.factsforprojects.com and clicking on the web link.

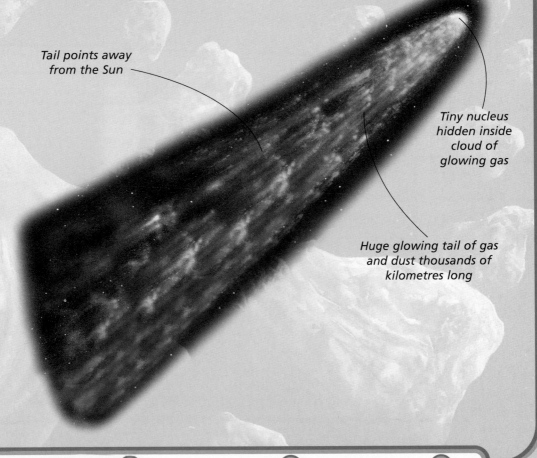

Tail points away from the Sun

Tiny nucleus hidden inside cloud of glowing gas

Huge glowing tail of gas and dust thousands of kilometres long

My naked eye ⬡   Binoculars ⬡   Telescope ⬡

SPACE ROCKS

FACT FILE

METEOR SHOWERS HAPPEN ON THESE DATES EVERY YEAR

Name	Date	Constellation
Quadrantids	3–4 Jan	Boötes
Perseids	12 Aug	Perseus
Orionids	21 Oct	Orion
Geminids	13 Dec	Gemini

SUPER FACT

During a meteor shower, all the meteors seem to come from the same place. Each shower is named after the constellation the meteors seem to come from.

PHOTO FILE

Most meteors are made by small pieces of space rock, about the size of a pea. Larger chunks make brighter fireballs.

MY NOTES & PICTURES

Date and time:

Where were you?

Who was with you?

Describe what you saw:

I HAVE...   Seen a meteor

Meteor Showers

They may look like stars shooting across the night sky, but shooting stars are not stars at all. They are streaks of light, made by small bits of dust or rock from space hitting the Earth's atmosphere. They move so fast that they burn up in the air. The streak lasts for only a few seconds and is called a meteor. The best time to look for meteors is during a meteor shower, when there may be one every few minutes. Meteor showers happen when the Earth travels through a trail of dust left behind a comet.

Complete a quiz and learn more about meteors by visiting www.factsforprojects.com and clicking on the web link.

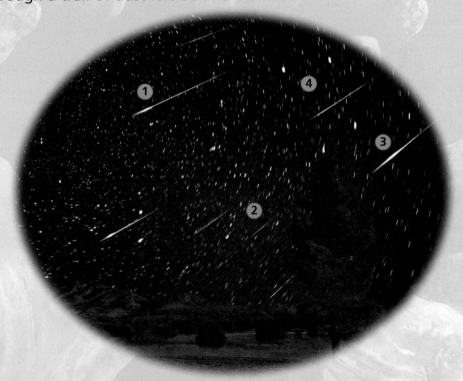

1 A meteor causes a quick flash of light

2 In a meteor shower, meteors may appear as often as one every minute

3 Some meteors are brighter than others

4 Meteors usually appear one at a time, but a photo taken during a shower can show many together

Watched a meteor shower ◯

SPACE ROCKS

FACT FILE

TYPES OF METEORITE

Stony Made mostly of rock
Iron Made mostly of iron mixed with another metal called nickel
Stony-iron A mixture of rock and iron
Mars/Moon Rock that has been chipped off the Moon or Mars

SUPER FACT

The largest meteorite was found in Namibia, in Africa. It is called the Hoba meteorite and weighs about 60 tonnes. This meteorite still lies where it was found in 1920.

PHOTO FILE

Fifty thousand years ago a meteorite crashed into Earth making Meteor Crater in Arizona, USA, which is 1.2 km wide.

MY NOTES & PICTURES

Date and time:
_____

Where were you?
_____

Who was with you?
_____

Describe what you saw:
_____
_____
_____

I HAVE SEEN...   **A stony meteorite**

Meteoroids and Meteorites

Pieces of rock and dust racing around the Sun in space are called meteoroids. They range in size from tiny specks of dust to large rocks. Meteoroids hit the Earth all the time, but most burn up in the Earth's atmosphere. Only the biggest fall to the ground and these are called meteorites. It is very rare to see a meteorite falling or even on the ground, so look for displays of them in museums.

Learn more about meteorites by visiting www.factsforprojects.com and clicking on the web link.

Iron meteorite

An iron meteorite is made of the metals iron and nickel

Smooth, shiny surface was melted when the meteorite heated up as it plunged into Earth's atmosphere

This stony meteorite is called a chondrite and is made of rock

Chondrite (stony) meteorite

Most meteorites found on Earth are stony meteorites

STARS

FACT FILE

BEST TIMES TO LOOK
Ursa Major February–May
Ursa Minor May–June
Cassiopeia October–December
Boötes May–June

SUPER FACT

The second star from the end of the Plough's handle, Mizar, is a double star with another star called Alcor. You may be able to see them both with the naked eye.

PHOTO FILE

The galaxy M81 is near the Pointers in Ursa Major. It has a distinctive spiral shape.

MY NOTES & PICTURES

Date and time:

Where were you?

Who was with you?

Describe what you saw:

I HAVE SEEN... Ursa Major Ursa Minor Cassiopeia

The Plough is a group of seven bright stars within the constellation Ursa Major. The seven stars form a saucepan shape when joined up. The two stars at the bottom of the Plough are called the Pointers. They lead to Polaris, the Pole Star, which marks the North Celestial Pole (see page 11). Follow a line from the Plough (1), past Polaris (2), to find the W shape of the constellation Cassiopeia. Look left along the 'handle' of the Plough (3) to an orange star, Arcturus, the brightest star north of the equator.

Find out which stars are visible each night by visiting www.factsforprojects.com and clicking on the web link.

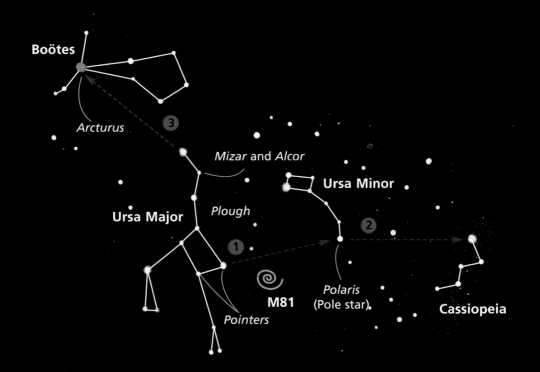

Boötes

Arcturus

3

Mizar and Alcor

Ursa Minor

Ursa Major

Plough

1

Ursa Major

M81

Polaris (Pole star)

2

Cassiopeia

Pointers

STARS

FACT FILE

BEST TIMES TO LOOK

Crux April–May

Centaurus April–June

Carina January–April

SUPER FACT

Alpha Centauri is really a group of three stars. One of these, Proxima Centauri, is the nearest star to the Sun, but you cannot see it with the naked eye.

PHOTO FILE

The supergiant star inside the Eta Carina Nebula may explode as a supernova. Look for a faint, reddish smudge near Crux.

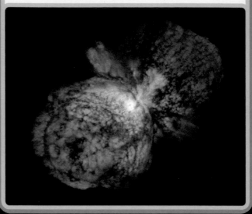

MY NOTES & PICTURES

Date and time:

Where were you?

Who was with you?

Describe what you saw:

I HAVE SEEN... Crux   Centaurus   Carina

Four bright stars in the shape of a small cross make up the constellation Crux. An imaginary line along its length (1) points to the South Celestial Pole, although there is no bright pole star. Two bright stars close to Crux are the Southern Pointers. They are the brightest stars, Alpha and Beta Centauri, in the constellation Centaurus. Follow a line from the Pointers (2), across the bottom of Crux, to the constellation Carina. Its brightest star is Canopus – the second brightest star in the sky.

Learn more about the constellations by visiting www.factsforprojects.com and clicking on the web link.

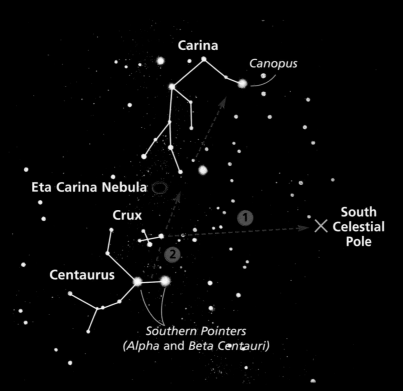

Carina

Canopus

Eta Carina Nebula

Crux

①

South
Celestial
Pole

②

Centaurus

*Southern Pointers
(Alpha and Beta Centauri)*

STARS

FACT FILE

BEST TIME TO LOOK

December–January

Can be seen from the Northern and Southern hemispheres.

If you live in the Southern Hemisphere, the pattern will appear upside down – the sword will be above the belt, Rigel will be at the top left and Betelgeuse will be at the bottom right.

SUPER FACT

Betelgeuse is about 500 times larger than the Sun and about 14,000 times brighter. If it replaced the Sun, it would swallow up all the planets to Mars, including Earth.

PHOTO FILE

Light from young stars makes the gas in the Orion Nebula glow, but the colours only show up through powerful telescopes.

MY NOTES & PICTURES

Date and time:

Where were you?

Who was with you?

Describe what you saw:

I HAVE SEEN...   Orion   Orion Nebula

Orion

The constellation Orion is one of the most recognizable in the night sky. Orion was a great hunter in Greek mythology. A line of three bright stars make up the hunter's belt. Below the belt is a smaller line of stars, the hunter's sword, with the fuzzy patch of the Orion Nebula in the middle. Binoculars show the shape of the nebula with its newborn stars. Two giant stars mark Orion's foot and shoulder – Betelgeuse is an old red giant (1) and Rigel is a younger blue giant (2).

Discover more about Orion's stars by visiting www.factsforprojects.com and clicking on the web link.

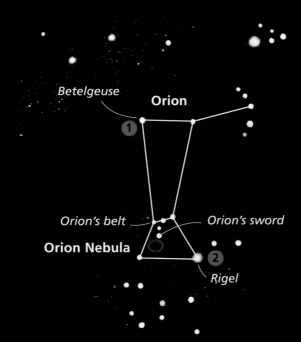

Orion is shown here in the Northern Hemisphere.

Betelgeuse 〇   Rigel 〇

STARS

FACT FILE

BEST TIME TO LOOK

Canis Major January–February

Gemini January–February

Canis Minor February

Can be seen from the Northern and Southern hemispheres.

If you live in the Southern Hemisphere, the patterns will appear upside down.

SUPER FACT

Castor looks like one bright star, but telescopes show a group of three stars. Each of these is also a double star, so Castor is actually a double double double star.

PHOTO FILE

The Eskimo Nebula is in the constellation Gemini. A dying star in the centre has thrown out rings of hot, glowing gas.

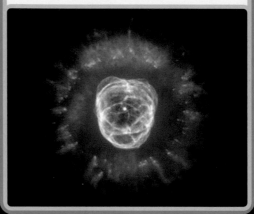

MY NOTES & PICTURES

Date and time:

Where were you?

Who was with you?

Describe what you saw:

I HAVE SEEN... Canis Major Gemini Canis Minor

Bright Stars near Orion

Sirius, in the constellation Canis Major, is the **brightest star in the sky.** Follow a line from Orion's belt (1), down to the left, to find Sirius. A line from Rigel (2), through the middle of Orion's belt, takes you up to the constellation Gemini. Its two brightest stars are Castor and Pollux. Moving left across Orion's shoulders from Betelgeuse (3), you can see the bright star Procyon, in the constellation Canis Minor. It makes a bright triangle in the winter sky with Betelgeuse and Sirius.

Watch a video about the stars near Orion by visiting www.factsforprojects.com and clicking on the web link.

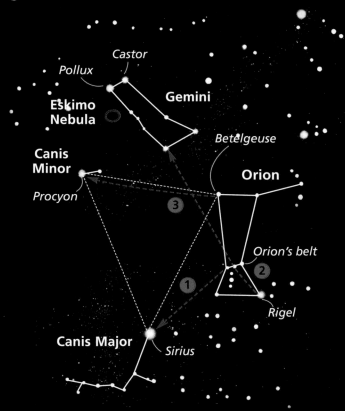

The bright stars near Orion are shown here in the Northern Hemisphere. If you live in the Southern Hemisphere, reverse the directions and follow the belt stars up to the right to find Sirius.

Sirius ◯   Castor ◯   Pollux ◯   Procyon ◯

FACT FILE

BEST TIME TO LOOK

Taurus December–January

Can be seen from the Northern and Southern hemispheres.

If you live in the Southern Hemisphere, the patterns will appear upside down.

SUPER FACT

The Crab Nebula, in the constellation Taurus, is the remains of an exploding star. Chinese astronomers saw the explosion nearly 1000 years ago in 1054.

PHOTO FILE

Telescopes show wisps around the stars of Pleiades. These are reflection nebulae – dust clouds reflecting the starlight.

MY NOTES & PICTURES

Date and time:

Where were you?

Who was with you?

Describe what you saw:

Taurus

Aldebaran, an old red giant star, marks the eye of the bull, Taurus. Follow a line up from Orion's belt (1) to find Aldebaran. Close to it is a V-shaped cluster of stars called the Hyades. You can see these clearly with the naked eye, but binoculars show even more stars. Follow the same line (2) to come to another bright cluster of young stars called the Pleiades. Look for about six stars with the naked eye and many more with binoculars.

Find out more about Taurus by visiting www.factsforprojects.com and clicking on the web link.

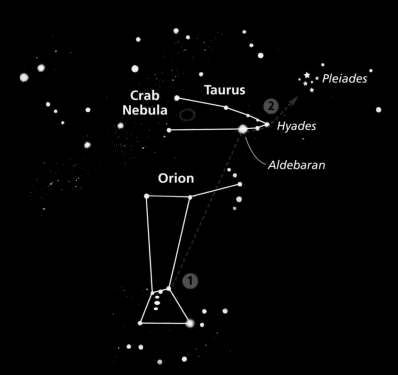

Taurus is shown here in the Northern Hemisphere. If you live in the Southern Hemisphere, reverse the directions and follow the belt stars down to the left to find Aldebaran.

Hyades ○   Pleiades ○

FACT FILE

BEST TIME TO LOOK

Lyra July–August

Aquila July–August

Cygnus August–September

The Summer Triangle is seen in the Northern Hemisphere in summer.

SUPER FACT

In 10,000 years time, the Earth will have tilted so that Vega will be nearer to the North Celestial Pole than Polaris is. It will become the pole star.

PHOTO FILE

The Ring Nebula is a planetary nebula near Vega. You might be able to pick it out as a fuzzy patch with binoculars.

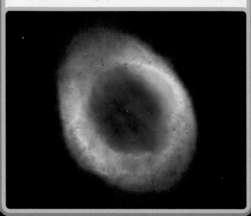

MY NOTES & PICTURES

Date and time:

Where were you?

Who was with you?

Describe what you saw:

I HAVE SEEN... Lyra Aquila Cygnus

The Summer Triangle

In the Northern Hemisphere summer sky, three bright stars mark the corners of the Summer Triangle. They are all from different constellations. The brightest star in the triangle is Vega (1), in the constellation Lyra. Altair is in the constellation Aquila (2) and Deneb is in the constellation Cygnus (3). Lyra and Aquila are not very bright, but you can see the swan shape of Cygnus. Deneb is the swan's tail. Its neck stretches to the middle of the Summer Triangle, with the wings on either side.

Watch a video about the Summer Triangle by visiting www.factsforprojects.com and clicking on the web link.

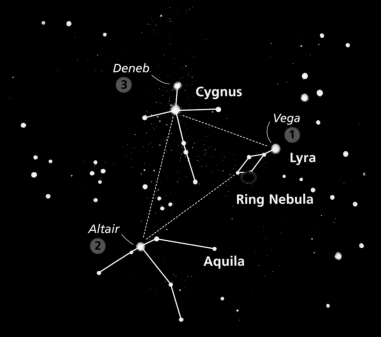

Deneb

3

Cygnus

Vega

1

Lyra

Ring Nebula

Altair

2

Aquila

STARS

FACT FILE

BEST TIME TO LOOK

Scorpius June–July

Sagittarius July–August

These constellations can be seen from the Southern Hemisphere.

SUPER FACT

When you look at Sagittarius, you are looking towards the centre of our Milky Way galaxy. The centre is hidden behind clouds of dust in the spiral arms of the galaxy.

PHOTO FILE

Telescopes show dark lines of dust in the glowing red gas of the Trifid Nebula. It is in Sagittarius, near the Lagoon Nebula.

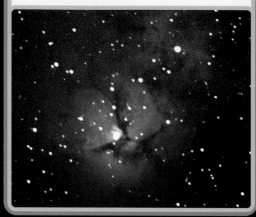

MY NOTES & PICTURES

Date and time:

Where were you?

Who was with you?

Describe what you saw:

I HAVE SEEN...　　Scorpius 　　Sagittarius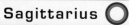

Scorpius

In the Southern Hemisphere sky, the constellation Scorpius is easy to recognize because it looks like a scorpion with a curled tail. Find it along a line from Crux, through the Southern Pointers (1). The bright red star in the middle of Scorpius, Antares, is a red supergiant star. Near the tail (2) is the teapot shape of the constellation Sagittarius. Look for the Lagoon Nebula near the lid of the teapot. You can just see it with the naked eye, but binoculars give a better view.

Discover more about Sagittarius by visiting www.factsforprojects.com and clicking on the web link.

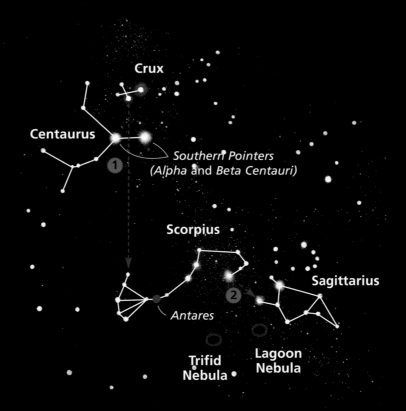

Crux

Centaurus

Southern Pointers
(Alpha and Beta Centauri)

1

Scorpius

Sagittarius

2

Antares

Trifid
Nebula

Lagoon
Nebula

GALAXIES

FACT FILE

Large Magellanic Cloud
Diameter 20,00 light years
Distance 157,000 light years

Small Magellanic Cloud
Diameter 10,000 light years
Distance 200,000 light years

These galaxies can only be seen from the Southern Hemisphere.
They are in the sky all year round.

SUPER FACT

The Large and Small Magellanic clouds were named after the Portuguese explorer Ferdinand Magellan, who spotted them in 1521, nearly 500 years ago.

PHOTO FILE

The Tarantula Nebula in the Large Magellanic Cloud is outside our galaxy, but it can be seen with the naked eye.

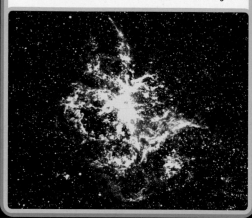

MY NOTES & PICTURES

Date and time:

Where were you?

Who was with you?

Describe what you saw:

I HAVE SEEN... Dorado   Tucana

Southern Hemisphere

The Large and Small Magellanic clouds are the nearest galaxies to the Milky Way. They look like cloudy patches in the sky. A line across the corner of Crux (1) leads to the Large Magellanic Cloud, which is mostly within the constellation Dorado. Look at it with binoculars to see brighter patches, which are nebulae or star clusters. A line down the length of Crux (2) points to the Small Magellanic Cloud, within the constellation Tucana.

Watch a video about the Magellanic clouds by visiting www.factsforprojects.com and clicking on the web link.

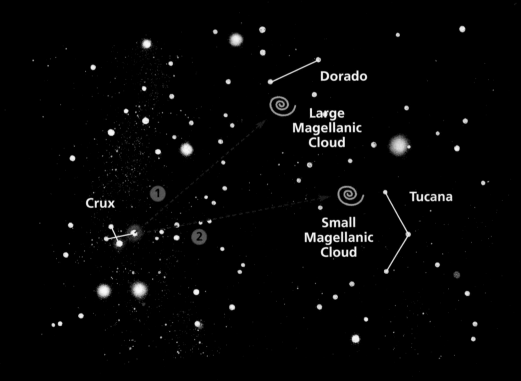

Dorado

Large Magellanic Cloud

Tucana

Crux

Small Magellanic Cloud

Large Magellanic Cloud ⬭ Small Magellanic Cloud ⬭

GALAXIES

FACT FILE

BEST TIME TO LOOK

October–February

Distance 2.3 million light years

Diameter 150,000 light years

The Andromeda Galaxy can be seen from the Northern Hemisphere.

SUPER FACT

The Andromeda Galaxy is on a collision course with the Milky Way. Billions of years from now they may pull each other apart and form a new, giant galaxy.

PHOTO FILE

The Andromeda Galaxy is a spiral galaxy, like the Milky Way. Large telescopes show spiral arms curling around a bright centre.

MY NOTES & PICTURES

Date and time:

Where were you?

Who was with you?

Describe what you saw:

I HAVE SEEN...   Pegasus ◯   Andromeda ◯

Andromeda

The most distant object you can see with the naked eye is the Andromeda Galaxy. Find it from the W shape of Cassiopeia. Follow a line between its centre-right stars (1), down to a large square with a star at each corner – the constellation Pegasus. Follow another line from the bottom-right corner of the square (2), back towards Cassiopeia. The Andromeda Galaxy is a fuzzy patch two-thirds of the way along. Binoculars show its oval shape and bright centre.

Learn to spot the Andromeda Galaxy by visiting www.factsforprojects.com and clicking on the web link.

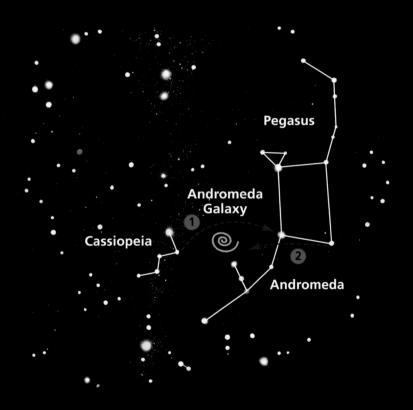

Pegasus

Andromeda Galaxy

Cassiopeia

Andromeda

GALAXIES

FACT FILE

Diameter 100,000 light years
Number of stars 200–400 billion stars
Distance of Sun from centre
25,000 light years
Shape Large spiral

SUPER FACT

The stars in the Milky Way are all orbiting around the centre of the galaxy. The Sun takes 226 million years to complete one orbit and we call this a galactic or cosmic year.

PHOTO FILE

The Milky Way is the light from stars in our galaxy. We cannot see its spiral shape because the Earth is inside the galaxy.

MY NOTES & PICTURES

Date and time: _____

_____

Where were you? _____

_____

Who was with you? _____

_____

Describe what you saw: _____

_____

_____

_____

I HAVE SEEN THE MILKY WAY WITH...

Milky Way

Our own galaxy, the Milky Way, looks like a very faint, uneven band of light across the sky. If you can find somewhere very dark, on a night when there is no Moon, you will be able to see the Milky Way. With binoculars you can see separate stars. The Milky Way is brightest in the Southern Hemisphere, in the winter, in the constellations Sagittarius and Scorpius. In the Northern Hemisphere, look for it in the constellation Cygnus, in the summer.

Discover more about the Milky Way by visiting www.factsforprojects.com and clicking on the web link.

Southern Hemisphere

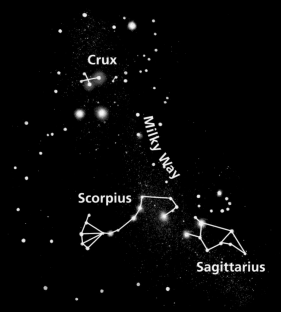

Crux

Milky Way

Scorpius

Sagittarius

Northern Hemisphere

Cygnus

Milky Way

Cassiopeia

FACT FILE

Height of Aurora At least 100 km

Colours Green or red – glowing oxygen
Pink or blue – glowing nitrogen

Shapes Arc – curved glow
Band – like a ribbon
Ray – vertical lines

Names Aurora Borealis – Northern Lights
Aurora Australis – Southern Lights

PHOTO FILE

From space, the Southern Lights make a glowing green ring around the South Pole. You can see Antarctica inside the circle.

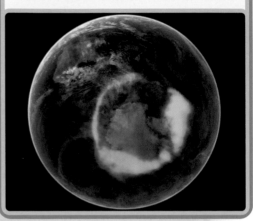

SUPER FACT

The Northern and Southern lights are brightest every 11 years, when there are the most sunspots on the Sun. This should happen in about 2013.

MY NOTES & PICTURES

Date and time: _____

_____

Where were you? _____

_____

Who was with you? _____

_____

Describe what you saw: _____

_____

_____

_____

_____

I HAVE SEEN THE...   Northern Lights

Northern and Southern Lights

The Northern and Southern lights (auroras) are glowing lights in the sky near the North or South poles. They happen when tiny atomic particles from the Sun plunge into the Earth's atmosphere, making the gases in the air glow. You can usually only see them from areas in the far North, such as Norway or Alaska, or in the far South, such as Antarctica. They look like moving green or red lights across the sky.

Look at pictures of the Northern Lights by visiting www.factsforprojects.com and clicking on the web link.

Dark sky above the forest trees

Shimmering green glow of the Northern Lights

Southern Lights

CLOSE TO EARTH

FACT FILE

Distance between Sun or Moon and halo, sundog or moondog
22° – about the width of two fists at arms length

Maximum height of sundogs in the sky
60° – two-thirds of the way from the horizon to overhead

SUPER FACT

The ice crystals that make halos and sundogs have six sides and they form in clouds 5–10 km up in the atmosphere.

PHOTO FILE

When you look at a halo around a Full Moon, the sky inside the bright ring often appears darker than the sky around it.

MY NOTES & PICTURES

Date and time:

Where were you?

Who was with you?

Describe what you saw:

I HAVE SEEN A... Sundog 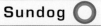 Moondog
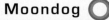

Halos and Sundogs

The air around the Earth often causes strange lights in the sky. A halo is a ring of light around the Moon or the Sun. This happens when they shine through a thin cloud made of ice crystals. The crystals bend some of the light, making a ring appear. Look for a halo around the Moon when it is full, or nearly full. Sundogs are patches of light like mini rainbows on either side of the Sun. They are also made by ice in the air. You can sometimes see moondogs on either side of the Moon.

See images of sundogs and moondogs by visiting www.factsforprojects.com and clicking on the web link.

Warning: Look for sundogs when the Sun is fairly low in the sky with thin clouds. Do not look at the Sun itself – block it out with your hand.

Halo

Sundog

Setting Sun

Sundog

FACT FILE

ORBITS OF THE INTERNATIONAL SPACE STATION AND IRIDIUM SATELITES

	ISS	Iridium
Height (km)	350	780
Time for one orbit of Earth (min.)	91	100
Number of orbits per day	15.7	14.4

SUPER FACT

The International Space Station takes only 1.5 hours to circle Earth. It travels through space at a speed of about 28,000 km/h, nearly 30 times faster than a jumbo jet.

PHOTO FILE

Iridium satellites send messages to satellite phones. Their large panels reflect sunlight, making a streak in the night sky.

MY NOTES & PICTURES

Date and time:

Where were you?

Who was with you?

Describe what you saw:

I HAVE SEEN...   A satellite ◯   An iridium flare ◯

Satellites

You can often see man-made satellites or the International Space Station orbiting Earth. They look like a slowly moving bright star high overhead. If you see one with flashing lights it is probably an aeroplane, not a satellite. Look for them soon after sunset when the sky is getting dark, but the satellite is still lit by the Sun. Satellites called iridium satellites spin around and make a bright flash as they reflect sunlight. These flashes are called iridium flares.

Find out when you will be able to spot the ISS by visiting www.factsforprojects.com and clicking on the web link.

Trail made by the International Space Station as it crosses the sky

These pages tell you where the 88 constellations are visible from – the Northern Hemisphere (N), Southern Hemisphere (S) or Northern and Southern hemispheres (N & S). They also tell you the best time to look for them.

	NAME	MEANING	WHERE	WHEN
	Lepus	Hare	N & S	Jan
	Auriga	Charioteer	N	Jan–Feb
	Canis Major	Great Dog	S	Jan–Feb
	Gemini	Twins	N & S	Jan–Feb
	Hydra	Sea Serpent	S	Jan–Feb
	Monoceros	Unicorn	N & S	Jan–Feb
	Puppis	Stern	S	Jan–Feb
	Lynx	Lynx	N	Jan–Mar
	Volans	Flying Fish	S	Jan–Mar
	Carina	Keel	S	Jan–Apr

NAME	MEANING	WHERE	WHEN
Canis Minor	Little Dog	N & S	Feb
Cancer	Crab	N & S	Feb–Mar
Pyxis	Compass	S	Feb–Mar
Vela	Sail	S	Feb–Apr
Ursa Major	Great Bear	N	Feb–May
Antlia	Air Pump	S	Mar–Apr
Leo	Lion	N & S	Mar–Apr
Leo Minor	Little Lion	N & S	Mar–Apr
Sextans	Sextant	N & S	Mar–Apr
Draco	Dragon	N	Mar–Sep
Crater	Cup	N & S	Apr
Canes Venatici	Hunting Dogs	N	Apr–May

NAME	MEANING	WHERE	WHEN
Columba	Dove	S	Apr–May
Coma Berenices	Berenice's Hair	N & S	Apr–May
Corvus	Crow	N & S	Apr–May
Crux	Southern Cross	S	Apr–May
Musca	Fly	S	Apr–May
Centaurus	Centaur	S	Apr–Jun
Virgo	Virgin	N & S	Apr–Jun
Boötes	Herdsman	N	May–Jun
Chamaeleon	Chameleon	S	May–Jun
Circinus	Compasses	S	May–Jun
Libra	Scales	N & S	May–Jun
Lupus	Wolf	S	May–Jun

	NAME	MEANING	WHERE	WHEN
	Ursa Minor	Little Bear	N	May–Jun
	Corona Borealis	Northern Crown	N & S	Jun
	Norma	Carpenter's Level	S	Jun
	Ara	Altar	S	Jun–Jul
	Ophiuchus	Serpent Bearer	N & S	Jun–Jul
	Scorpius	Scorpion	S	Jun–Jul
	Triangulum Australe	Southern Triangle	S	Jun–Jul
	Hercules	Strongman	N & S	Jun–Aug
	Serpens	Serpent	N & S	Jun–Aug
	Apus	Bird of Paradise	S	Jul
	Aquila	Eagle	N & S	Jul–Aug
	Corona Australis	Southern Crown	S	Jul–Aug

	NAME	MEANING	WHERE	WHEN
	Lyra	Lyre	N	Jul–Aug
	Sagittarius	Archer	S	Jul–Aug
	Scutum	Shield	N & S	Jul–Aug
	Telescopium	Telescope	S	Jul–Aug
	Pavo	Peacock	S	Jul–Sep
	Sagitta	Arrow	N & S	Aug
	Capricornus	Sea Goat	N & S	Aug–Sep
	Cygnus	Swan	N	Aug–Sep
	Delphinus	Dolphin	N & S	Aug–Sep
	Microscopium	Microscope	S	Aug–Sep
	Vulpecula	Fox	N & S	Aug–Sep
	Aquarius	Water Carrier	S	Aug–Oct

NAME	MEANING	WHERE	WHEN
Indus	Indian	S	Aug–Oct
Equuleus	Foal	N & S	Sep
Cepheus	King	N	Sep–Oct
Grus	Crane	S	Sep–Oct
Lacerta	Lizard	N	Sep–Oct
Pegasus	Winged Horse	N & S	Sep–Oct
Piscis Austrinus	Southern Fish	N & S	Sep–Oct
Tucana	Toucan	S	Sep–Nov
Octans	Octant	S	Oct
Andromeda	Chained Princess	N	Oct–Nov
Phoenix	Phoenix	S	Oct–Nov
Pisces	Fishes	N & S	Oct–Nov

NAME	MEANING	WHERE	WHEN
Sculptor	Sculptor	S	Oct–Nov
Cassiopeia	Queen	N	Oct–Dec
Cetus	Whale	N & S	Oct–Dec
Hydrus	Water Snake	S	Oct–Dec
Eridanus	River Eridanus	S	Nov–Jan
Aries	Ram	N & S	Nov–Dec
Fornax	Furnace	S	Nov–Dec
Horologium	Clock	S	Nov–Dec
Perseus	Hero	N	Nov–Dec
Triangulum	Triangle	N & S	Nov–Dec
Reticulum	Net	S	Dec
Caelum	Chisel	S	Dec–Jan

	NAME	MEANING	WHERE	WHEN
	Dorado	Goldfish	S	Dec–Jan
	Orion	Hunter	N & S	Dec–Jan
	Taurus	Bull	N & S	Dec–Jan
	Mensa	Table Mountain	S	Dec–Feb
	Pictor	Painter's Easel	S	Dec–Feb
	Camelopardalis	Giraffe	N	Dec–May

FINDING OUT MORE

Astronomy clubs

One of the best ways to become a space detective is to join your local astronomy club. Your local library may be able to tell you where the nearest one is. In the UK, many astronomy clubs are listed on the website of the Federation of Astronomical Societies:
http://www.fedastro.org.uk/fas/

Other useful astronomy organizations

The Society for Popular Astronomy: **http://www.popastro.com/**
The British Astronomical Association: **http://britastro.org/baa/**

Astronomical magazines

Many astronomy magazines have star charts showing what's in the sky each month. They also provide information about where to look for planets and other interesting objects.
Astronomy
Astronomy Now
Popular Astronomy
Sky and Telescope
Sky at night

Websites

Try these websites for lots of interesting information and facts about space and astronomy, games, pictures and things to do:

http://nasascience.nasa.gov/kids
http://spaceplace.jpl.nasa.gov/en/kids/
http://starchild.gsfc.nasa.gov/docs/StarChild/StarChild.html
http://www.nasa.gov/audience/forkids/kidsclub/flash/index.html
http://www.esa.int/esaKIDSen/
http://www.astronomy.com/asy/default.aspx?c=ss&id=127

These websites have star charts showing the sky each night, as well as other useful information:
http://popastro.com/youngstargazers/thismonth.html
http://schoolsobservatory.org.uk/
http://www.space.com/nightsky/
http://popastro.com/
http://www.skyviewcafe.com/skyview.php
http://www.astronomy.com/asy/stardome/default.aspx